CONTROLLING
INVASIVE SPECIES
WITH GOATS

BY CAROL HAND

CONTENT CONSULTANT
Katherine M. Marchetto
Post-Doctoral Associate, College of Veterinary Medicine
University of Minnesota

Core Library

An Imprint of Abdo Publishing

Cover image: Goats can be an effective tool in fighting

abdocorelibrary.com

Printed in the United States of America, North Mankato, Minnesota
012019
092019

THIS BOOK CONTAINS RECYCLED MATERIALS

Cover Photo: Linda Davidson/The Washington Post/Getty Images
Interior Photos: Linda Davidson/The Washington Post/Getty Images, 1, 4–5, 29, 45; Oswalt CM, Fei S, Guo Q, Iannone III BV, Oswalt SN, Pijanowski BC, Potter KM (2015) A subcontinental view of forest plant invasions. NeoBiota 24:49–54, 7; iStockphoto, 9, 14, 17; Ronnie Chua/Shutterstock Images, 11, 34–35, 43; Timothy S. Allen/Shutterstock Images, 12–13; Evan Frost/Minnesota Public Radio/AP Images, 20–21; Timothy Yue/Shutterstock Images, 26–27; Caleb Whitmer/The Holland Sentinel/AP Images, 30; Red Line Editorial, 36; Jim Marabello/Worcester Telegram & Gazette/AP Images, 38

Editor: Marie Pearson
Series Designer: Ryan Gale

Library of Congress Control Number: 2018964504

Publisher's Cataloging-in-Publication Data

Names: Hand, Carol, author.
Title: Controlling invasive species with goats / by Carol Hand.
Description: Minneapolis, Minnesota : Abdo Publishing, 2020 | Series: Unconventional science | Includes online resources and index.
Identifiers: ISBN 9781532118982 (lib. bdg.) | ISBN 9781532173165 (ebook) | ISBN 9781644940891 (pbk.)
Subjects: LCSH: Invasive species--Juvenile literature. | Alternative agriculture--Juvenile literature. | Goats--Juvenile literature. | Environmental protection--Juvenile literature. | Weeds--Biological control--United States--Juvenile literature.
Classification: DDC 578.62--dc23

CONTENTS

CAN GOATS SAVE THE ENVIRONMENT?

Andy is a tall goat. He often eats standing on his hind legs. He can eat plants more than eight feet (2.4 m) high. Andy loves many kinds of plants, including poison ivy, thorny roses, and bittersweet. He is part of a herd of 70 goats known as the Eco Goats. They work along the East Coast of the United States. They eat invasive plants. These are non-native plants that grow so fast they become a nuisance.

Brian Knox owns Eco Goats. He says goats provide a simple solution to the problem of

Goats eat many kinds of invasive plants, even those that are hard to reach.

invasive plants. He rents his goat herds by the week. They clean up overgrown vegetation. A herd of 35 goats can eat approximately half an acre (0.2 ha) of vegetation in four days. By then, they are tired of that food and ready to move on. Knox loads them onto a trailer. He moves them to a new location with a new type of food. Knox says, "I joke that I drive the bus, but they're the real rock stars."

WHY GOATS?

Goats are an ideal way of controlling invasive plants. They enjoy eating plants humans want removed. They graze in places machines can't go, such as steep, rocky hillsides. Pulling plants by hand is difficult, but goats often pull them to eat. Herbicides are toxic and dangerous. Machines are noisy. They use harmful fossil fuels. They also pack down the soil. This makes it less able to soak up water. With goats, pesticides and machines can be unnecessary.

PLANTS TAKING OVER

Invasive plants are overtaking native plants across the United States. Sometimes humans plant the invasive seeds. Other times wind or

US INVASIVE PLANT
MAP

This map gives results of a 2016 study by the US Forest Service. It shows the percentage of forested land having at least one invasive species. Where in the United States do forests have the greatest invasive plant problem? Why do you think these regions have more invasive plants than others?

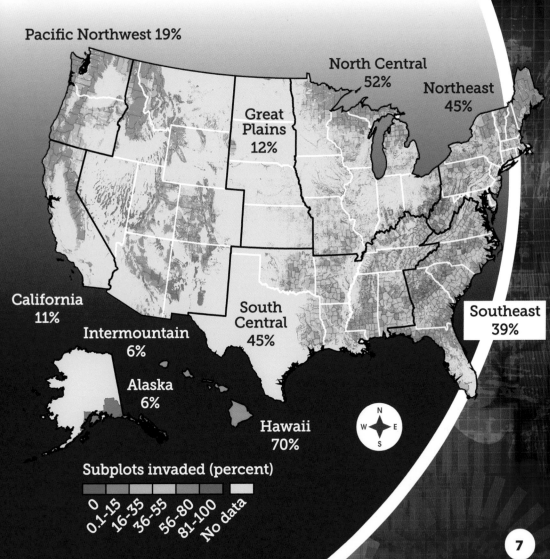

Pacific Northwest 19%

North Central 52%

Northeast 45%

Great Plains 12%

California 11%

Intermountain 6%

South Central 45%

Southeast 39%

Alaska 6%

Hawaii 70%

Subplots invaded (percent)

0 0.1-15 16-35 36-55 56-80 81-100 No data

animals may carry these seeds into new environments. The invasive plants take over rapidly. This happens because they produce many seeds or have fast-growing root systems. Many invasive plants grow well in disturbed soil. This includes roadsides or soil plowed for agriculture.

Invasive plants damage native plants. They may grow faster and take over habitats. Their thick root systems may smother the roots of native plants. Some invasive plants produce chemicals. The chemicals prevent native plants from growing. Native plant diversity declines as invasive plants take over. The US Forest Service calls invasive plants a critical threat to forests and grasslands. They are also a danger to agriculture. Farmers can lose billions of dollars when invasive weeds destroy crops.

STOPPING INVASIVE PLANTS

US land managers use several methods to stop invasions of non-native plants. In small areas, they may pull or dig

Controlled burns can help kill off invasive species. They clear the way for native species to grow again.

out the plants. In larger areas, plants are cut or mowed. But this does not kill the roots. They must be mowed for several years. People often use toxic herbicides, or plant-killing chemicals. The most common herbicide is nonselective. This means it kills all kinds of plants. Sometimes, people control plants with fire. This is called prescribed burning. Burning is strictly controlled. It requires a permit.

BREEDS OF GOATS

There are approximately 200 breeds of goats. Different breeds are suited for different purposes. Nubian and Saanen goats are bred to produce milk. Boers and kikos are common types bred for meat. Angora goats have long soft wool called mohair. Cashmere goats are bred for their cashmere wool. All goat breeds like to browse and graze. So all can be used for vegetation control.

Goats are a biological control method. So far, they are mostly used by government agencies. These include counties, cities, and more than a dozen states. The goats eat many unwanted plants. They are useful in areas where mowers cannot reach. Goats graze on hillsides and some parts of cities. They fertilize the soil as they eat. They are nontoxic, and they are fun to watch. Goats are environmentally friendly.

Sometimes goat farmers use horses to help control goat herds.

Goats were once commonly used to control weeds and shrubs. Modern methods such as mowing and chemicals replaced them. But goats may be making a comeback. More people are realizing that goats can be useful. They have advantages over machines and chemicals. People are beginning to use goats as one more tool to control invasive plants.

THE INVASIVE PLANT PROBLEM

Kudzu is known as "the vine that ate the South." This Asian plant was introduced into the southeastern United States in 1876. It was meant to shade homes and control erosion. But the southeast has a warm climate. There, kudzu grows up to one foot (0.3 m) a day. It quickly took over. It smothers buildings and trees. Kudzu is an invasive plant. Invasive plants are not native to an area. They grow faster than native plants. They may harm the environment or human health. They may destroy crops or damage buildings. Repairs cost money.

Kudzu can kill trees and damage power lines.

Invasive species, such as purple loosestrife, may look pretty, but they do a lot of damage to some habitats they are not native to.

WHICH PLANTS ARE INVASIVE?

Kudzu is one of thousands of invasive plants in the United States. It is one of the country's top six most invasive plants. Others are purple loosestrife, Japanese honeysuckle, Japanese barberry, Norway maple, and English ivy. Invasive plants can be noxious.

This means they are harmful to people or habitats. State governments try to control them and prevent their spread. Pastures and rangelands have both invasive plants and noxious weeds. Landowners want noxious weeds removed. Many are thorny or prickly plants. These include red cedar, multiflora rose, thistles, and buckthorn. Autumn olive, smartweed, and poison ivy are other unwanted plants. Phragmites, an invasive reed, lives in salt marshes.

The most successful plant invaders produce many seeds. They grow

GOATS' FAVORITE INVASIVE FOODS

Many of goats' favorite foods are plants that people consider pests. Goats are not bothered by toxins in plants such as poison ivy. They happily chomp on thorny plants, such as multiflora rose, buckthorn, blackberry, and thistles. They love fast-growing invasives such as kudzu and mile-a-minute weed. Other favorites are English ivy, spotted knapweed, and phragmites. Goats prefer woody plants over non-woody plants.

rapidly. They readily adapt to changing conditions. These plants make it difficult for native plants to compete for resources. They displace native plants and change the environment.

WHY ARE INVASIVE PLANTS HARMFUL?

Invasive plants change the amount of water and food particles in the soil. They change light and temperature levels. These changes affect growing conditions. Native plants die or get pushed out. Some invasive plants increase fires in an area. Others increase soil erosion or change the way nutrients move between plants and animals. Changes vary based on the type of plant. Changes also depend on the original habitat.

Controlling invasive plants is expensive. Weed control costs the United States billions of dollars per year. But not controlling weeds is more expensive. The Weed Science Society of America (WSSA) says that if left uncontrolled, weeds would destroy about half

Herbicides are the most common way to keep weeds from destroying crops.

of corn and soybean crops. This would cost farmers approximately $43 billion a year.

The WSSA thinks only herbicides can save crops. It says farmers must use herbicides wisely. This will prevent weeds from becoming resistant to herbicides. If weeds are herbicide-resistant, more herbicide is required to kill them. Experts recommend using a combination of methods to fight weeds. One method is

WHY NOT HERBICIDES?

Herbicides are often used to kill invasive plants. However, herbicides are toxic. They kill or damage native plants too. They seep into water and soil. There, they are picked up by both plants and animals. They may cause tumors in animals such as deer. They also make humans ill. There are strict safety guidelines for herbicide use. Professionals must follow the guidelines. But private homeowners and community groups often do not.

rotating crops between different fields. Planting different crops in the same field in different years helps kill weed seeds. It can also help destroy weed roots. Another is changing how soil is prepared for use. This includes covering soil with black plastic, which kills weed seeds.

Most experts still prefer herbicides for controlling weeds or invasive plants in crop fields. But goats are often a better choice on pastures, rangelands, and hilly or rocky areas. Goats also have advantages in parks, cities, and natural areas such as woodlands and prairies.

STRAIGHT TO THE
SOURCE

Penny Perkins is an ecological restoration specialist for Practical Farmers of Iowa (PFI). She studied goats' ability to help restore land damaged by invasive species. She made the following observations during the two-year study:

"The plots that had been browsed were visibly clearer, more open and easier to walk through. The control plots were very, very dense with vegetation at the end of the study." . . . But, she observed honeysuckles coming back in the browsed plots. "To successfully use goats to control invasive woody species, you need to flash graze at a high enough stock density to completely defoliate an area." The point of flash grazing is [to] get livestock to eat the plants quickly, sapping the reserves within the plant.

Penny does not think that two browsing periods within the same year is enough to fully kill undesirable plants.

Source: PFI Cooperators' Program. "Using Goats to Control Invasive Species." *Practical Farmers of Iowa,* December 2016. Web. Accessed October 10, 2018.

Back It Up
Read the passage carefully. Determine the main idea of the text. List two or three details that support the main idea.

THE GOAT SOLUTION

Goats are not a new answer for controlling invasive plants. Goats were domesticated, or tamed, about 9,000 years ago. They have controlled vegetation in the United States for at least 120 years. Some experts think they will be used much more in the future.

How Do Goats Work?

Animals that eat woody plants, or brush, are called browsers. Goats are mostly browsers. They eat the leaves of shrubs and thorny plants. Goats also like vines, such as poison ivy and honeysuckle. Sometimes goats are grazers. Grazers eat non-woody plants such as grasses.

Goats eat weeds that many other animals will not.

Goats graze on forbs rather than grasses. Forbs are broadleaved, non-woody plants such as dandelions.

Goats can be stubborn but are usually easy to control. Goat renters usually keep the goats inside electric fences. The fences can be moved to different locations. The goats are trained to load onto trucks or trailers. Many goat farmers also use herding dogs, such as border collies, to help move the goats. Farmers and dogs stay with the goats 24 hours a day. This helps keep the goats safe.

Goat farmers set up browsing plans. They figure out the

CAUSING PROBLEMS

Goats can cause problems when controlling invasive plants. They may also eat native plants. They may damage trees. If no leaves are available, they will eat tree bark. This can kill the trees. After goats have eaten the right amount of invasive plants, they must be removed quickly. Otherwise, they may destroy too many native plants.

best times for goats to remove invasive plants. They try to choose times when flowers and seeds are present. Controlling the plants may require several years of browsing.

HOW EFFECTIVE ARE GOATS?

Goats' mouths make them effective browsers. Their mouths are narrow and triangular. They grind their food with circular motions. This means they crush the food. Crushing destroys seeds. The goats' digestive systems further destroy them. Seeds that pass through a goat's gut cannot sprout. They cannot form new plants. Also, goat waste is good fertilizer. As goats walk, they stomp the waste into the ground. Goats can graze or browse all day.

Goats eat plants that sheep and cattle ignore. If they are hungry, they may eat plants they would otherwise ignore. But they prefer plants they have eaten before. This means they may need time to adjust to a new food plant.

COSTS VARY

The cost of goat browsing varies. In Ventura County, California, goats clear brush to prevent fires. If firefighters did the work, it would cost five times more. Goats browse every year in a wetland along a Maryland highway. These goats cost about the same as other control methods. But sometimes goats are too expensive. Goats used in a Salem, Oregon, park cost the city $20,719 for six weeks. Mowers run by prison inmates would cost only $3,370 to $4,425.

GOAT COSTS

Farmers who rent goats must charge a lot to stay in business. Often, other farmers and ranchers cannot afford to pay this much. So goat farmers usually work for public agencies. These include cities, governments, and highway departments. Some breeds of goats are raised for meat.

Goat farmers may rent goats to clear invasive plants. Later, they sell the goats for meat. These farmers are more likely to make a profit.

Cities and governments need less-costly ways to control invasive plants. They also want to protect

the environment. They are especially worried about herbicides. These groups often turn to goats. One goat rental company is Steel City Grazers of Pittsburgh, Pennsylvania. They charge a fee of $300 plus $5 to $10 per goat per day. Smaller goats eat less, so they cost less.

Goats are not always useful for plant control. Other methods are used in crop fields. But often, goats are the best choice. Their use requires little or no technology. It requires little or no equipment and fossil fuels. Usually, herbicides are not used either. Because they are low-tech, goats are friendly to the environment.

EXPLORE ONLINE

Chapter Three talks about how goats effectively control invasive species. The article at the website below goes into more depth on this topic. Does the article answer any of the questions you had about using goats to control invasive species?

GRAZING GOATS HELP CONTROL INVASIVE WEED SPECIES
abdocorelibrary.com/controlling-invasive-species-with-goats

CHAPTER
FOUR

WHO USES GOATS?

Goat grazing businesses are becoming more common. Grazing when plants first invade can prevent them from getting established. It may control already established plants. When goats destroy the leaves and seeds, plants cannot spread. Goats may also stop invasive plants from overtaking native plants. But usually goat grazing cannot completely remove plants from an area.

WHERE AND WHY?

Sometimes goats graze the same area over several years. Each year the number of invasive plants decreases. Fewer goats are

City parks are a common place where goats work to control invasive species.

needed. Sometimes people combine goat grazing with mowing. Cities and county governments hire goats to graze roadsides and natural areas such as parks or woodlands. Ranchers and farmers sometimes use them. Even airports and schools use goat grazers.

People who hire goats almost always want to avoid using dangerous herbicides. And other methods may not work in a location. For example, Pittsburgh's hills make mowing difficult.

HOW THE PUBLIC VIEWS GOATS

Goats fascinate people. Many people love to watch goats at work. Jacob Langeslag owns Goat Dispatch in Minnesota. He says goats are a lot of fun. Homeowners have cookouts and invite friends to watch his goats browse. Goats are friendly, and children enjoy petting them. But in one Salem, Oregon, city park, people complained about the smell of the goats' waste.

Heavy machinery damages wetland soil. Areas around buildings may be too small or steep for mowers. So the city recruits goats for the job.

People often enjoy watching goats at work.

CITY AND COUNTY PARKS

Trail manager Linda Moran works on the Polly Ann
Trail in Oakland County, Michigan. In 2017, she hired
goats to browse on buckthorn, a shrub with long
thorns. They also ate invasive reeds. They ate a vine

Signs encourage people not to pet or feed goats so the goats can stay safe and work more effectively.

that was smothering trees along the trail. Moran says the goats control plants safely. Visitors enjoy them too. Minneapolis and Saint Paul, Minnesota, hired goats to control the spread of invasive plants. The plants included multiflora rose, buckthorn, and honeysuckle. The goats worked at lakeside parks and along the Mississippi River.

Chimney Rock State Park in North Carolina has a kudzu problem. Goats are the solution. In 2015, approximately 15 goats spent two weeks eating in an area overrun with kudzu. David Lee arranged the goat grazing. Lee works for the Carolinas Mountain Land Conservancy, a conservation group. Goats control kudzu invasions cheaply. No chemicals are needed.

FROM RANCHES TO AIRPORTS

The Washoe Tribe owns Stewart Ranch in Carson Valley, Nevada. The tribe uses goats to remove rabbit brush. They once used herbicides. But the weeds became herbicide-resistant.

WHERE ARE GOATS APPROPRIATE?

Goat grazers may not fit all situations. Sometimes goats eat native plants instead of invasive ones. In Washington State, goats did a good job eating weeds in a fenced area. But they did not do well clearing a roadside or a freeway. They were less contained and did not stay on task. Sometimes, goats are too expensive. They do not clear enough plants to be worth their cost.

Also, herbicides ran off into local streams. Restoring the land with goats takes several years. But the results are worth it. As the land improves, native animals are returning. There are more deer, antelope, egrets, and bears.

Even airports use goats. Chicago's O'Hare International Airport uses a herd of goats, sheep, llamas, and burros. Each animal likes different plants. The mixed herd controls all types of invasives. Machines cannot be used on approximately 120 acres (50 ha) of airport land. Using grazers and browsers prevents pollution. The airport burns less gasoline in mowers. They do not spray herbicides.

Goats are making a comeback. People are rediscovering how helpful goats are in vegetation control. They may not be useful everywhere. But in the right situations, they are extremely effective.

STRAIGHT TO THE
SOURCE

The Adkins Arboretum in Maryland is devoted to native tree conservation. On its website, the arboretum explains why goats are a good choice for weed control:

Goats are sure-footed browsing animals with an appetite for a wide variety of plants, including thorny, woody plants that many other animals will not eat. Using goats to repeatedly graze an area will kill most woody plants without using herbicides or mechanical means of control. Goats can also be used to quickly clear away brush for access to pursue other treatment methods. . . . A herd of about 30 goats can clear a half-acre [0.2 ha] area in about two days.

Source: "Goats for Weed Control at Adkins Arboretum." *Adkins Arboretum.* Adkins Arboretum, n.d. Web. Accessed September 27, 2018.

Changing Minds

Decide whether you think goats or herbicides would be best for brush removal. Assume your friend has the opposite opinion. Write a short essay trying to change your friend's mind. Give your opinion and your reasons, including supporting facts.

RESEARCH AND THE FUTURE

G oats can help control invasive and noxious plants. But are goats really important in plant control? Or are they just a fad? Some people think goats will have an important role in the future. They are convinced goat grazing is here to stay.

RECENT RESEARCH

Scientists are researching the value of goats to control plants. They have shown that goat diets vary by location. Goats in Virginia reduced multiflora rose by 98 percent over five years. On western rangelands, goats preferred about 43 percent browse (including leaves, bark, and stems), 45 percent grass, and 12 percent forbs.

Goats may be used to control weeds even more in the future.

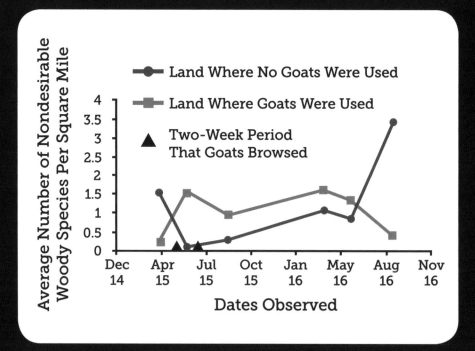

Scientists let goats browse in areas with invasive plants. Goats browsed for two two-week periods (shown by black triangles). The first browsing period began May 13; the second began June 27. No goats browsed in control areas. Study the graph. Did goats help control woody invasive plants? How can you tell?

A study in Wisconsin showed that goats preferred 82 to 88 percent brush and wood and ate only 3 percent grass.

Cherrie Nolden works at the University of Wisconsin–Madison. She studied types of grazing and browsing. In mob grazing, many goats are used to browse an area for a short period of time. Mob grazing is useful because the goats are less likely to wander and search for favorite foods. They will graze an area more evenly. In rotational grazing, handlers move the herd from place to place. Goats do not graze one area continuously.

They return to an area several times. When an invasive plant grows back, they remove it on the next pass.

Researchers at the University of Georgia are studying laws relating to goats. Most city laws do not consider goats. The researchers want city planners and goat farmers to work together. Researchers should figure out the number

INTEGRATED WEED MANAGEMENT

State and county weed specialists help Kansas landowners control and eliminate weeds. They use a process called integrated weed management. This combines various methods, including mowing and chemicals. It includes goats as a biological control method.

Goat farmers check their goats regularly to make sure they are healthy.

of goats needed. They should develop grazing plans for different situations. They should describe fencing and other tools needed to maintain and control goats. They should consider public health and safety.

FUTURE RESEARCH

So far, knowledge of goats' effectiveness mostly comes from people's experiences. There are few studies. No one is sure how long the benefits last or how much money they save. People need information on situations where goats should not be used. Also, goats grazing in the Midwest and East often pick up a parasite. This worm does little damage to deer, its primary host. But the worm spends part of its life in snails. Goats sometimes eat snails when grazing. The worm then enters goats' brains. There are few treatment options. It often kills them.

The University of Minnesota is planning a large study on goats as weed control. It will consider the benefits and issues. A team of scientists at the university will study how effective the goats are at controlling buckthorn and the effects the goats have on native plants. They will look

WHEN GOATS CAUSE DESTRUCTION

Project Isabela ran from 1997 to 2006. Its goal was to restore several of the Galápagos Islands, off the coast of Ecuador. Goats destroyed these islands. People once brought goats to the islands. The goats bred, and their numbers grew. Northern Isabela Island had more than 100,000 goats. The goats destroyed the native vegetation. Like any farm animal, goats must be controlled. Their population must not grow too large for the area.

into a method that could reduce the risk that goats will be infected with the deadly parasite. Dr. Stephen Kania of the University of Tennessee will develop a test to see if goats are infected with this parasite. Then the goats can be treated before the parasite begins hurting them. Researchers expect many benefits from the study. Today, how effective goats are at damaging invasive plants is based on opinions rather than facts. The study will provide landowners with more information about how much the goats help and their effects on native plants. This way, landowners can make better decisions about how to control invasive plants.

THE FUTURE OF GOATS

Goats seem like a natural choice for plant control. More people now realize this. The demand for goat grazers is growing. Mary Powell of Kansas started a goat ranch in 2012. In 2016, she began renting her goats as grazers. Her company, Barnyard Weed Warriors, helps the environment. She also saves money on feed.

Powell shares her knowledge with other women. She thinks goat grazing will take off.

The scientific study of goat grazing is just beginning. But stories like Powell's suggest that studies will prove goat grazing's benefits. It will not replace herbicides or mowers. So far, it is only being used in about a dozen states. But goats are highly useful in natural areas. They can work in places where mowers can't reach and herbicides are dangerous. Goats can help with invasive plant control. Goat grazers are likely here to stay.

FURTHER EVIDENCE

Chapter Five discusses the future of goats in weed control. Identify its main point and list several key pieces of evidence supporting that point. Then visit the website below. Find a quotation in the article that supports the chapter's main point. Does this quotation support a piece of evidence from the chapter? Or is it a new piece of evidence?

HERDERS AND GOATS HELP WYOMING FIGHT INVASIVE WEEDS
abdocorelibrary.com/controlling-invasive-species-with-goats

FAST FACTS

- Invasive plants are overtaking vegetation in the United States today. Invasive plants are non-native. They often grow faster than native plants.

- Land managers have several ways of controlling invasive plants. These include physical methods such as digging or mowing. They also include chemical methods such as herbicides.

- Goats are a biological method of invasive plant control. Goats are environmentally friendly. People who graze goats use little or no herbicides. They use fewer or no fossil fuels for mowing.

- Controlling invasive plants is expensive. But not controlling them is even more expensive. Invasive plants will overtake forests and destroy food crops.

- Grazers eat non-woody plants, including grasses and forbs. Sheep and cattle are grazers. Browsers eat woody and thorny plants. Goats are browsers. But goats also graze.

- Goats are effective browsers. They crush seeds, so the seeds will not sprout after passing through a goat's digestive system.

- Some goat farmers are now renting out goat herds by the day or week to clean up or control invasive vegetation.

- Goats can prevent invasive plants from getting established. They can control or suppress plants. But they seldom remove invasives entirely.

- About a dozen states are using goats to graze or browse vegetation. Often, goats are used in parks and other natural areas. They are used in steep areas where mowing is not possible.

- If grazing location and timing are not well controlled, goats may eat native plants as well as invasives. They may also overgraze or overbrowse an area, damaging the habitat.

- There have been few studies on the value of goats in controlling invasive plants. New studies are now being done or have been proposed. Thus, better evidence will soon be available.

- It is likely that goat grazing to control invasive plants will increase in the future.

STOP AND
THINK

Tell the Tale

Chapter One discusses Andy and other goats that eat invasive plants along the East Coast. Imagine a park with native trees, shrubs, and non-woody plants. The park also has rapidly growing invasive plants, including kudzu, discussed in Chapter Two. Suppose park managers do not control the kudzu. Write 200 words describing what you think would happen to the park over several years, and why.

Surprise Me

Chapter Three discusses the use of goats to control invasive plants. What two or three facts about goats and their uses were most surprising to you? Write a few sentences about each fact. Why did these facts surprise you?

Dig Deeper

After reading this book, what questions do you still have about using goats to control invasive plants? With an adult's help, find a few reliable sources that can help you answer your questions. Write a paragraph about what you learned.

Say What?

Studying land management and control of invasive plants means learning some new vocabulary. Find five words in this book you've never heard before. Use a dictionary to find out what they mean. Then write the meanings in your own words and use each word in a sentence.

GLOSSARY

browser
an animal such as a goat or deer that feeds on the leaves or bark of trees and shrubs

diversity
a measure of the number of species, or types, of living things present in an area

domesticated
tamed so as to be able to live and work with humans

established
to have taken root and begun growing and multiplying

forb
a broad-leaved, non-woody plant, such as a dandelion or clover

fossil fuel
natural gas and other fuels that have formed underground from the remains of plants and animals

grazer
an animal such as a cow or sheep that feeds on grasses and forbs

herbicide-resistant
having become tolerant to herbicides and less likely to die when sprayed with herbicide

vegetation
all the plants in an area

weed
a plant growing where it causes damage or is not wanted; often used to describe an invasive plant

ONLINE RESOURCES

To learn more about controlling invasive species with goats, visit our free resource websites below.

Core Library
CONNECTION
FREE! COMMON CORE MULTIMEDIA RESOURCES

Visit **abdocorelibrary.com** or scan this QR code for free Common Core resources for teachers and students, including vetted activities, multimedia, and booklinks, for deeper subject comprehension.

Booklinks
NONFICTION NETWORK
FREE! ONLINE NONFICTION RESOURCES

Visit **abdobooklinks.com** or scan this QR code for free additional online weblinks for further learning. These links are routinely monitored and updated to provide the most current information available.

LEARN MORE

Gaines, Alison. *Invasive Plants and Birds.* New York: Cavendish Square, 2017. Print.

Weaver, Sue. *Mini Goats.* Irvine, CA: i-5 Publishing, 2016. Print.

INDEX

About the Author

Carol Hand grew up on a farm and has owned goats. Now she is a freelance science writer. She has written more than 50 science and technology books for young people. She has degrees in zoology, including a PhD in marine biology.